THE CENTRAL WALES LINE

• A PAST AND PRESENT COMPANION •

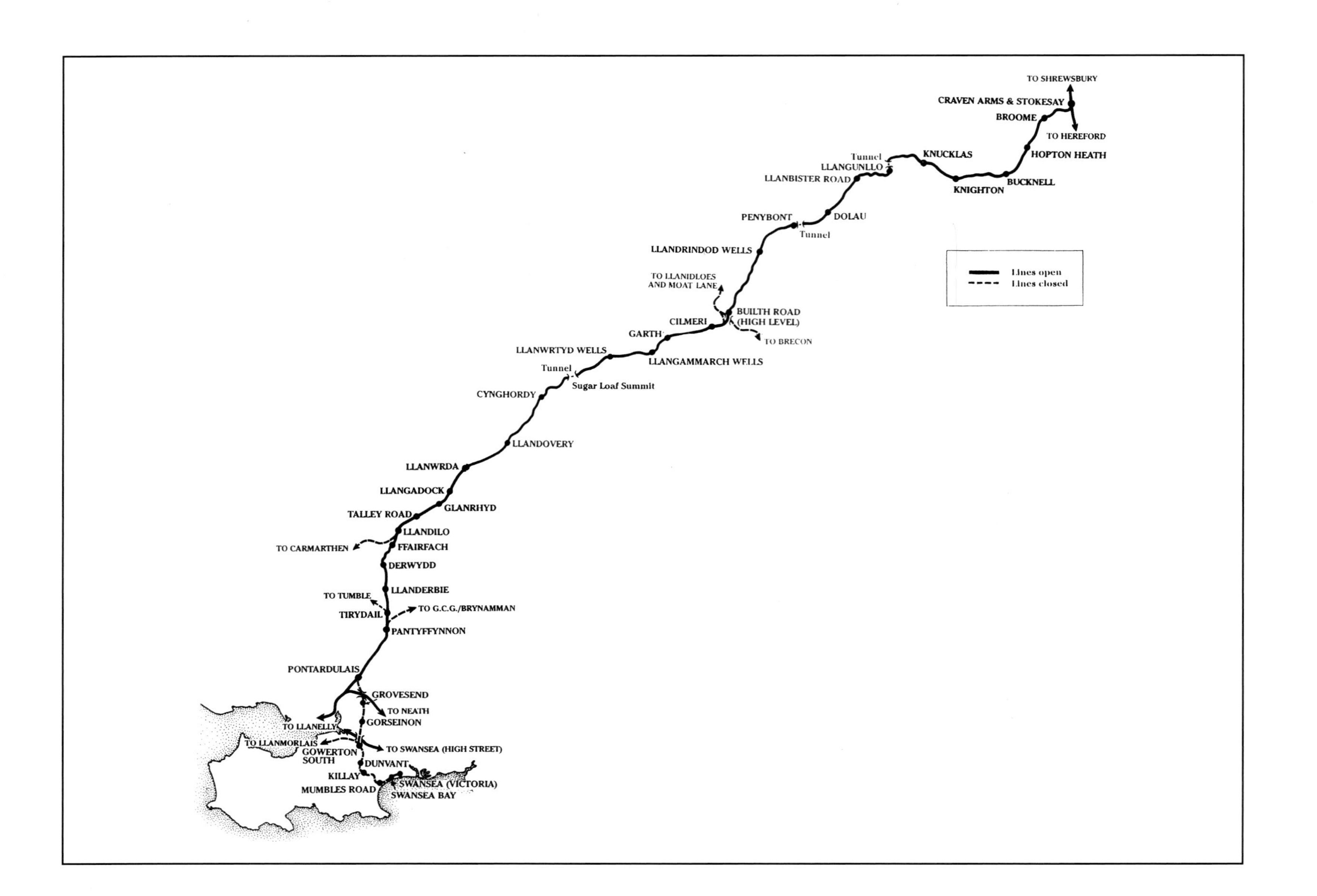
TO SHREWSBURY
CRAVEN ARMS & STOKESAY
BROOME
TO HEREFORD
HOPTON HEATH
BUCKNELL
KNIGHTON
KNUCKLAS
Tunnel
LLANGUNLLO
LLANBISTER ROAD
DOLAU
Tunnel
PENYBONT
LLANDRINDOD WELLS
Lines open
Lines closed
TO LLANIDLOES
AND MOAT LANE
BUILTH ROAD
(HIGH LEVEL)
TO BRECON
CILMERI
GARTH
LLANGAMMARCH WELLS
LLANWRTYD WELLS
Tunnel
Sugar Loaf Summit
CYNGHORDY
LLANDOVERY
LLANWRDA
LLANGADOCK
GLANRHYD
TALLEY ROAD
LLANDILO
TO CARMARTHEN
FFAIRFACH
DERWYDD
LLANDERBIE
TO TUMBLE
TO G.C.G./BRYNAMMAN
TIRYDAIL
PANTYFFYNNON
PONTARDULAIS
GROVESEND
TO NEATH
TO LLANELLY
GORSEINON
TO LLANMORLAIS
TO SWANSEA (HIGH STREET)
GOWERTON
SOUTH
DUNVANT
KILLAY
MUMBLES ROAD
SWANSEA (VICTORIA)
SWANSEA BAY

THE CENTRAL WALES LINE

• A PAST AND PRESENT COMPANION •

A nostalgic trip along the whole route from Craven Arms to Swansea

Roger Siviter ARPS

• RAILWAY HERITAGE •
from
The NOSTALGIA *Collection*

First published in 1999
Reprinted 2008

British Library Cataloguing in Publication Data

A catalogue record for this book is available from the British Library.

ISBN 978 1 85895 138 6

Past & Present Publishing Ltd
The Trundle
Ringstead Road
Great Addington
Kettering
Northants NN14 4BW

Tel/Fax: 01536 330588
email: sales@nostalgiacollection.com
Website: www.nostalgiacollection.com

Printed and bound in the Czech Republic

Past and Present

A Past & Present book
from
The* NOSTALGIA *Collection

ACKNOWLEDGEMENTS

I should like to thank the following people for their help in compiling this book, without whom it would not have been possible:

Lens of Sutton
Hugh Ballantyne
Ben Ashworth
F. W. ('Tim') Shuttleworth
Allan Sommerfield
All the photographers credited herein
My wife Christina
The staff at Past & Present Publishing Ltd
The railwaymen who made it possible

And finally all the many people who kindly allowed me access to their land in order to obtain that elusive 'present' picture.

BIBLIOGRAPHY

Portrait of the Central Wales Line by Martin Smith (Ian Allan)
A Regional History of the Railways of Great Britain,
Volume II – North & Mid Wales by Peter Baughan (David & Charles)
Forgotten Railways, Volume II – Severn Valley & Welsh Border by Rex Christiansen (David & Charles)
The Railway Magazine
Trains Illustrated

CONTENTS

The first station in Wales travelling south on the Central Wales Line is at Knucklas, 15½ miles from Craven Arms. Just beyond the station is the 13-arch Knucklas viaduct, built in stone and crossing the Heyope valley. This view at Knucklas was taken on 5 June 1964 and shows the timber-built station and the viaduct with its castellations just beyond. The view from this point today is almost entirely obscured by trees, but the station is still there and now has a new waiting shelter complete with 'old style' canopy, as do many of the stations on this attractive route. *B. J. Ashworth*

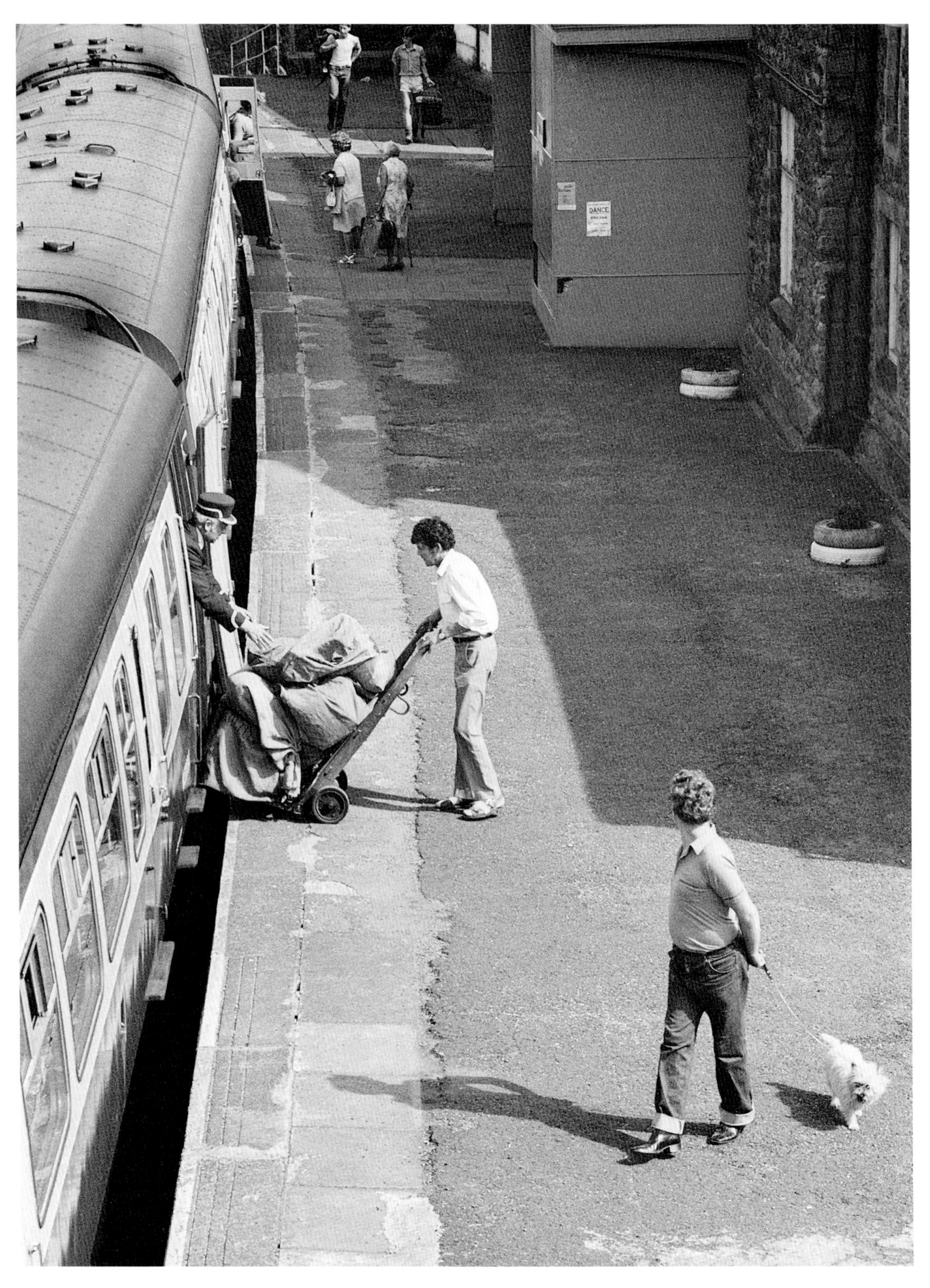

On 12 August 1983 a three-car DMU set forming the 1227 Swansea to Shrewsbury train pauses at Knighton, not only for passengers but also for a fair amount of mail. Worthy of note is the guard's British Rail uniform. *Roger Siviter*

INTRODUCTION

In August 1952 I was spending a week's holiday at Littlehampton and, during that time, spent a day at Brighton where there were many second-hand book shops. While browsing through the books at one of these shops, I came across several pre-war bound volumes of *The Railway Magazine*, priced, if my memory serves me correctly, at £1 10s per volume. Although I was not yet 16 and still at Grammar School, I was by then earning 'a few bob' playing trumpet on gigs with local dance bands, so I was able to purchase six volumes from 1936 to 1938 – there were two volumes per year in those days.

They were fascinating volumes to read, especially the inauguration of the East and West Coast streamlined trains, the LNER's 'Coronation' and the LMS's 'Coronation Scot', both with handsome record-breaking streamlined 'Pacific' locomotives in charge. On the GWR there were the exploits of the famous 'Castle' Class 4-6-0s on the 'Bristolian', with a 105-minute schedule for the 117.6 miles from Paddington to Bristol, and of course the luxury Pullman trains on the Southern Railway, as well as that company's famous 'Atlantic Coast Express'. Surely this was the heyday of British railways.

By now you will be wondering what this has to do with the Central Wales line. Amongst all these articles and pictures of famous trains, one article intrigued me above all else. This was in the September and October 1938 issue, and was headed 'London-Swansea via LMSR'. This not only gave a short history of the line but also described a journey over the line from Shrewsbury to Swansea. When the article was written, the 'Manxman', which left Euston on Mondays to Fridays at 10.40am, included a through coach to Swansea that ran to Shrewsbury via Stafford; together with coaches from Manchester and Liverpool, it then left Shrewsbury at 2.40pm for Swansea via Craven Arms and the Central Wales Line, arriving at 6.35pm, a total mileage from Euston (via Stafford) of 280 miles. On Saturdays, the through coach was attached to the 'Welshman' (11.05am from Euston) for its journey to Swansea. For the return journey, the Euston coach was attached to the 7.45am from Swansea.

The fare for this lengthy and interesting journey was governed by that of the GWR Paddington to Swansea (High Street) route – only some 199 miles. So with the inter-availability of a monthly return ticket, it was possible to travel to Swansea via the GWR and return via the LMS, and of course vice versa.

Since that day in 1952 in a Brighton bookshop, when I first became aware of the Central Wales line, I have visited the area on many occasions, and have enjoyed not only the lovely scenery through which the line passes, but also the hospitality of the people who live there.

Today, the Central Wales route reaches Swansea (High Street) via Llanelly, the Pontardulais-Swansea (Victoria) section having been closed in 1964. However, for the purposes of this book, we travel on the old route, the original Central Wales Line.

Roger Siviter
Evesham

In glorious evening sunlight Nos 80079 and 44767 head north out of Craven Arms with a Carmarthen to Shrewsbury special, after a fine run over the Central Wales Line on 6 June 1993. *RS*

Craven Arms to Llandrindod Wells

Our journey down the Central Wales Line begins at Craven Arms, some 95 miles from Swansea (Victoria). Craven Arms was not only the junction for the Central Wales and North to West routes, but there was also a locomotive shed at the north-western end of the station, which had amongst its duties the Central Wales Line. This former London & North Western Railway (LNWR) shed was, together with Knighton and Builth Road, a sub-shed of Shrewsbury, and closed in the mid-1960s. Outside the shed on a snowy 20 February 1955 are ex-LNWR 0-6-2T No 58904, a design introduced in 1882, and ex-Midland Railway 0-6-0 No 58207 of 1878. Inside the shed were Class '2F' 0-6-0s Nos 58213 (with tender cab) and 58203, ex-LNWR Class '6F' 0-8-0 No 49033, Fowler 2-6-2T No 40008, and Stanier 2-6-2T No 40105, with an 87K plate.

Today's scene, taken on 17 February 1998, shows the site of the old shed with only an out-of-use siding for comparison. *F. W. Shuttleworth/RS*

45145

CRAVEN ARMS AND STOKESAY
JUNCTION FOR LLANDRINDOD WELLS
AND CENTRAL WALES LINE

The first view of Craven Arms & Stokesay station shows ex-LMS 'Black Five' 4-6-0 No 45145 pulling out of Craven Arms with an afternoon Shrewsbury to Swansea (Victoria) train on 31 March 1962.

The second photograph was taken on 16 August 1968, again looking towards Shrewsbury, and shows the fine-looking station nameboard, the closed bay platform on the left, which had an overall roof, and in the distance a DMU departing for Shrewsbury. Craven Arms was also the terminus for the Bishops Castle Railway, which closed in 1935, and for the line from Much Wenlock, which closed to passenger traffic in 1951 (see *British Railways Past and Present Special: The Severn Valley Railway*).

The present view of Craven Arms was taken on 17 February 1998 and shows 'Sprinter' unit No 158839 leaving the station with the 1133 Manchester (Piccadilly)-Cardiff service. A comparison with the two earlier pictures shows that the old station buildings have been replaced by 'bus shelters' and the new footbridge is nearer to the middle of the station. On the left-hand side can be seen the old goods shed (now out of use) and also some disused sidings. Some semaphore signals still remain, as does the signal box at the crossing north of the station. Note the facing crossover, just north of the station, for use by Central Wales Line trains. *Hugh Ballantyne/J. A. Sommerfield/RS*

Class 33 diesel No 33021 heads south from Craven Arms with the 1320 Crewe-Cardiff train on 12 August 1983. The Central Wales Line can be seen coming in from the right-hand side. Note the ground frame on the extreme right and the semaphore signal controlling entry to the Central Wales Line. Both Swansea and Shrewsbury trains use the northbound platform, the Swansea train gaining access to it via the crossover seen in the previous picture just north of the station.

On 17 February 1998 we see the rear of unit No 158831 as it leaves with the 1138 Manchester-Cardiff service. The ground frame and Central Wales semaphore have gone, and the new notice on the right says 'Start of token section to Knighton'. This 12¾-mile section was originally double-track, but was singled in 1965. *Both RS*

Two and a half miles from Craven Arms, the first station on the Central Wales route is Broome, and this view of the station, taken probably around 1900, is looking towards Shrewsbury. The station buildings were all of wood, as were the signal box and the Swansea platform. In line with many of the stations on the route, Broome also had a small goods yard, here on the west side of the line.

Today the Central Wales Line, apart from passing loops, is all single-track. This view of Broome, taken on 20 March 1998, shows that all that remains of the old station is the platform itself. Just above the end of the platform can be seen the chimneys of the cottages seen in the earlier view. *Lens of Sutton/RS*

This view of Hopton Heath (5½ miles from Craven Arms), looking south, was taken in LMS days before 1945, when the signal box in the picture was removed and a new one placed just south of the station on the Swansea side.

Today's view, taken on 20 March 1998, shows just a single track through the station. The station house and old goods shed are in very good order and are now in private use. The remains of the northbound platform can also still be seen. *Lens of Sutton/RS*

Although still in Shropshire as far as Knighton, after leaving Craven Arms the line passes through the historic and beautiful area known as the Welsh Marches. Before reaching the border town of Knighton, the line runs through Bucknell, where it meets the River Teme, which follows the line as far as Knucklas, some 7 miles from Bucknell and 15½ miles from Craven Arms. This view of the station, looking north, was taken around the turn of the century and shows the fine station buildings, and the goods shed and yard just beyond the crossing gates.

The main station house is still there in the 'present' picture, taken on 20 March 1998, but traffic lights now control the crossing and a new passenger shelter in the 'old style' has been installed. The old northbound platform is still there, complete with attractive flower beds. Although the goods yard has long gone, the goods shed survives, but, like the station house, is in private use. *Lens of Sutton/RS*

C813

We have now reached the market town of Knighton, 12¾ miles from Craven Arms, and these three views show the changes that have taken place over the years. The first, taken around the early part of the century, is looking towards Craven Arms. Note the goods yard and what look like private-ownership goods sheds, and also the ornate station buildings.

On 12 August 1983 the 1227 Swansea-Shrewsbury DMU waits to depart from Knighton. The goods yard has now gone, but some of the sheds remain with some now additions. There is just single track through the station, but the old northbound platform seems in reasonable order.

The 'present' view, taken in 20 March 1998, shows that there has been something of a transformation at Knighton. The double track has been put back and the northbound platform re-instated, with new shelters added. The train waiting to leave is the 0910 Swansea-Shrewsbury service formed of unit No 153377. *Lens of Sutton/RS (2)*

Just to the east of Knighton station was the small locomotive shed, seen here on 20 February 1955, looking towards Craven Arms. Although there were no locomotives on shed at the time, it was usually home to smaller engines for working local traffic.

This is the site of the shed on 20 March 1998, with only the single track and hillside to provide a comparison with the 'past' picture. *F. W. Shuttleworth/RS*

Water stop at Knighton on 2 June 1964, as BR Standard Class '4MT' 2-6-4T No 80069 replenishes its tanks while working the 2.40pm Shrewsbury to Swansea (Victoria) train.

The scene is repeated on 13 October 1997 as preserved ex-LMS 2-6-0 No 2968 takes water from a hydrant while working a Swansea to Shrewsbury special charter.

Before leaving Knighton, it is worth noting that although the station is in England the town is actually in Wales; just over a mile west of the station the line also enters Wales for the rest of the journey to Swansea. *B. J. Ashworth/RS*

Four miles after passing through Knucklas, 15½ miles from Craven Arms (see also page 5), we reach Llangunllo station. This view, taken on 14 May 1966, shows the two platforms – Llangunllo was a passing place and originally had a small goods yard.

Today the station houses are in private use, and only one platform and line remain, but for all that the small station looks trim with a new shelter and smart iron railings. *Michael Mensing/RS*

Llanbister Road station – which served the village of Llanbister, 4 miles from the station – is our next location. The first picture shows the station in LMS days. Note the small goods yard just beyond the station, and the signal box and lower-quadrant signals, which date the picture to probably around 1930.

The second picture was taken only a few years ago, on 23 May 1993, but shows a rare event, a southbound Class 37 diesel plus coach. Normally, apart from the odd excursions, only DMUs have worked the route, but this short train was following up a steam special.

Obviously, many things have changed since LMS days. There is now only one track through the station, and no goods yard or signals, etc, and the station house is in private use. Today's view, dated 20 March 1998, shows that the 'bus shelter' in the previous photograph has gone, to be replaced by a smart-looking shelter in the 'old style'. These stations are a credit to the 'Heart of Wales Line' that now operates the route. *Lens of Sutton/RS (2)*

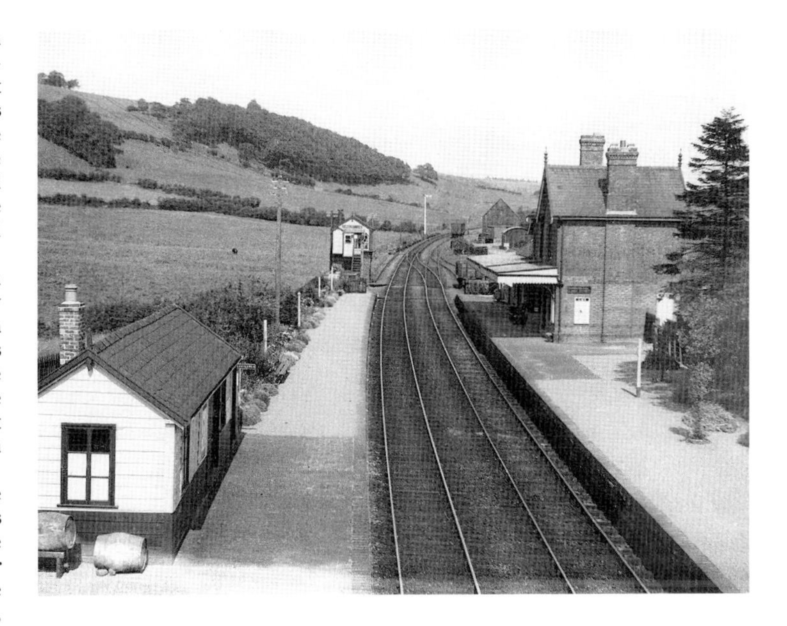

Some 3 miles from Llanbister Road and nearly 26 miles from Craven Arms is Dolau station. Although this view, looking towards Craven Arms on 9 August 1971, shows the track now to be single through the station, the signal box and old-style crossing gates are still there – they went in 1975 when an unmanned level crossing was installed.

On 20 March 1998 single-car unit No 153377 approaches Dolau with the 1311 Shrewsbury-Swansea service. The station looks smart and tidy, complete with flower beds and benches, and the old northbound platform is now a trim lawn. *J. A. Sommerfield/RS*

On 6 June 1964 Standard Class 5 4-6-0 No 73025, with the 1210 Swansea (Victoria) to Shrewsbury train, pauses to surrender the single-line token at the start of the double-track section just north of Penybont Tunnel. Note the white sighting board, which was to provide drivers with a clearer view of the home signal located in the cutting near the tunnel mouth.

At the same location on 7 March 1998 we see the rear of a Paddington-Swansea-Craven Arms-Paddington excursion, hauled by Class 47 diesel No 47744. The newly refurbished coaching stock is in 'Southern Green'. *B. J. Ashworth/RS*

Turning to look the other way, we see the front view of No 73025 as it leaves the northern portal of the 402-yard-long Penybont Tunnel, and also No 47744 in the same location. This excursion was organised by Hertfordshire Railtours. *B. J. Ashworth/RS*

After leaving Penybont Tunnel, the line runs through Penybont station, nearly 29 miles from Craven Arms. On 14 May 1966 a Llanelly-bound Swindon 'Cross Country' DMU, minus its middle coach, leaves Penybont station with the 2.50pm from Shrewsbury and heads south for its next stop at Llandrindod Wells. Just south of the tunnel the line had been double-track again, but was singled at the end of 1965, as the photograph clearly shows.

On 7 March 1998 we see the rear of single unit No 153377 as it approaches Penybont station with the 1223 Swansea-Shrewsbury service. The sidings have now gone and the main line has been centred on the double trackbed. *Michael Mensing/RS*

One of the most important towns served by the Central Wales/Heart of Wales Line is Llandrindod Wells – not only the county town of Powys but also a famous Victorian spa town, set in one of the most beautiful and unspoilt parts of Wales, where its origins go back to Roman times. It has many attractions, amongst which are the National Cycle Exhibition, the Albert Hall Theatre and the Pavilion Conference Centre, to name but a few; these, together with elegant shops and many fine hotels and guest houses, make it a excellent centre for holidays. On 16 May 1964 ex-LMS Class '8F' No 48471 heads through the station with a northbound freight. The line through the station was singled in 1955.

Today the northbound line has been re-instated as this view, taken on 7 March 1998, shows. The train is the rear of the 1311 Shrewsbury-Swansea service comprising single unit No 153380. We are some 32 miles from Craven Arms, and the journey will have taken 58 minutes; the train will arrive at Swansea at 1657, having taken 3 hours 46 minutes for the 121 miles from Shrewsbury to Swansea via Llanelly. The original route, which is the subject of this book, was 95¾ miles from Craven Arms to Swansea (Victoria), Craven Arms being 20 miles from Shrewsbury. A comparison between the two pictures shows many differences, but the main station building is still the same. The station was refurbished in the Victorian style in the early 1990s, the northbound platform having been re-opened for passenger use in 1986. North of the station there was a goods yard, but this was closed many years ago. *B. J. Ashworth/RS*

Ex-LMS 'Jubilee' Class 4-6-0 No 45577 *Bengal* pulls into Llandrindod Wells on the morning of 5 June 1964 with the 7.25am Swansea (Victoria) to Shrewsbury train. From 1963 these attractive 4-6-0s were regular performers on the Central Wales Line, *Bengal* being amongst the most active.

Nowadays, in place of a 'Jubilee' we have single-car unit No 153380, waiting to head south with the 1440 to Swansea (1311 from Shrewsbury). This view shows the new footbridge and canopies and, beyond the train, the signal box just beyond which the line reverts to single track. *B. J. Ashworth/RS*

Builth Road

Just under 6 miles from Llandrindod Wells is Builth Road (High Level) a fascinating railway location where the Central Wales Line crossed over Builth Road Low Level station on the Mid Wales Line from Moat Lane Junction on the Shrewsbury-Machynlleth line to Three Cocks Junction on the Hereford to Brecon line. (For further details of the Mid Wales route see *British Railways Past & Present No 32: Mid Wales and the Marches.*) The accompanying map provides a guide to this somewhat unusual railway location.

The first picture, dated 4 June 1964, shows ex-LMS Class '5' 4-6-0 No 45145 heading north out of the High Level station with an afternoon Swansea (Victoria)-Shrewsbury train; the crew are just about to take the token for the single-line section to Llandrindod Wells.

On 7 March 1998 very little remains from the previous scene. All the sidings, signals and signal box have gone, although the goods shed remains in commercial use. *B. J. Ashworth/RS*

HIGH LEVEL

LOW LEVEL

BUILTH ROAD

SHED

On 7 June 1960 ex-LMS Fowler 2-6-4T No 42390 takes water at High Level station before leaving with the 7.40am Craven Arms-Swansea (Victoria) train. There is much to enjoy in this picture, not least the splendid station nameboard; note also the directions to the Low Level station.

This was the scene at Builth Road on 7 March 1998. In the distance is the rear of the 0910 Swansea-Shrewsbury service formed of single unit No 153380. The station house is still there in good order and now used as a private dwelling. *Hugh Ballantyne/RS*

The train seen in the 'past' picture on page 28 is seen here again approaching the High Level station on 4 June 1964, while waiting to head south is ex-LMS '8F' 2-8-0 No 48328 and its crew. Prominent on the left-hand side is the lift connecting the High Level with the Low Level station.

On 7 March 1998 unit No 153380 approaches Builth Road station with the 0910 Swansea to Shrewsbury service. Note the smart railings on the left. *B. J. Ashworth/RS*

46511
LADIES ROOM
STATION MASTER'S OFFICE
BOOKING OFFICE & WAITING ROOM

BUILTH ROAD
LOW LEVEL
CHANGE FOR
LLANDRINDOD, LLANWRTYD
LLANGAMMARCH &c
BOOKING OFFICE & WAITING ROOM
LADIES ROOM
CATCH POINTS

Ex-LMS 2-6-0 No 46511 enters Builth Road Low Level station with a Moat Lane to Brecon train on 24 August 1962, a few months before closure. By 20 May 1964, the date of the second picture, the line is closed but the track, etc, is still in situ to permit the demolition contractors, Thomas Ward, to bring recovered materials from Builth Wells to the goods yard here at Builth Road. Crossing the High Level bridge is '8F' 2-8-0 No 48444 with a goods train, heading towards Craven Arms.

The 'present' view of the site of the Low Level station was taken on 7 March 1998. The old refreshment room is now a pub, and the waiting rooms are now private dwellings, with additional dormer windows, etc. Behind the photographer the station area is now used as a garage and workshop. *B. J. Ashworth/Hugh Ballantyne/RS*

We are now looking south from the northbound platform of the High Level station on 4 June 1964, as Standard Class 5 4-6-0 No 73090 leaves with a Swansea (Victoria) train. On the right-hand side can be seen the line connecting the High Level and Low Level stations; also, in the distance can be seen the tiny locomotive shed and goods yard.

On 7 March 1998 single unit No 153308 heads south at Builth Road with the 0855 Shrewsbury to Swansea service. Apart from the single track, everything has now gone. This picture also shows how the northbound platform was formerly extended across the small overbridge. *B. J. Ashworth/RS*

On 29 August 1962 Class '2MT' 2-6-0 No 46508 is seen shunting coal wagons in the small yard near the attractive locomotive shed. On 7 March 1998 the whole area is a timber yard, and only the background hills correspond with the 'past' picture. *B. J. Ashworth/RS*

Interlude: preserved steam on the Central Wales Line

Since 1993, quite a few steam specials have traversed the Central Wales route, and the following pictures show a selection of the specials at various locations on the line.

Above **A panoramic view of Knucklas and the surrounding countryside, as ex-LMS 'Black Five' 4-6-0 No 44767 and Standard Class 4 2-6-4T No 80079 head for Craven Arms and Shrewsbury with a special charter train from Carmarthen on 6 June 1993.** *RS*

Right **After an absence of nearly 30 years, steam returned to the Central Wales Line on 16 May 1993, when 2-6-4T No 80079 headed a Shrewsbury to Carmarthen train. The special is seen climbing the 1 in 101 bank on what used to be the double-track section just south-west of Bucknell.** *RS*

80079

The following Sunday, 23 May 1993, saw another special from Shrewsbury to Carmarthen, this time headed by 4-6-0 No 44767. The first picture shows the train at speed east of Knighton, where it stopped to take water, while the second shows the special crossing the impressive Knucklas viaduct. *Both RS*

On 23 October 1993 2-6-4T No 80079 and sister engine No 80080 make an imposing sight as they climb the 1 in 60/70 up to Sugar Loaf Tunnel with a charter from Pantyffynnon to Shrewsbury. This location is a few yards south of the 1,001-yard tunnel. *RS*

Former LMS 'Mogul' No 2968 is seen approaching and departing from Knighton on the early evening of 18 October 1997. The locomotive paused at Knighton to take water (see the picture on page 19). *Both RS*

The final picture in this section shows a special on what is today the final section of the Central Wales route, from Llanelly to Swansea. The location is the 1 in 60 out of Swansea (formerly High Street) station on the line to Llanelly and Carmarthen. Heavy rain adds to the atmosphere as 4-6-0 No 44767 heads for Carmarthen (then Tenby and Fishguard) on the early morning of 30 May 1993. On the left is the line to Paddington. *RS*

Over Sugar Loaf to Llandilo

After leaving Builth Road the line runs through Cilmery, which had an unstaffed halt that closed in the 1950s, then calls at Garth, just over 43 miles from Craven Arms. This view of Garth station (looking north) was taken on 9 April 1972, by which time the southbound platform had been closed and the line singled through the station. Garth was originally used as a passing place, and at one time possessed a small goods yard.

By 26 April 1998, although the old station buildings have gone, they have been replaced by the new 'old-style' shelter now common to this route. Note also the flower beds and bushes, etc. *J. A. Sommerfield/RS*

Just under 2 miles south of Garth is Llangammarch Wells station. The station only ever had one platform, but, like Garth, had a small goods yard. By the time that this 'past' picture was taken (looking south) on 9 April 1972, the yard was closed.

Today's view, taken on 26 April 1998, shows that a new waiting room has replaced the old one, and also that the station has a new nameboard. *J. A. Sommerfield/RS*

Since Penybont, the line has roughly followed the valley of the River Irfon, but just south of the next station, Llanwrtyd Wells, it crosses the water as the river swings northwards towards its source in the Cambrian mountains. Just arriving at Llanwrtyd Wells station on 8 February 1975 is the 1225 Swansea (High Street) to Shrewsbury train.

Apart from a few additions on the platform, etc, not a lot appears to have changed over the 23 years separating the two pictures. Today's view was taken on 26 April 1998. *Michael Mensing/RS*

After leaving Llanwrtyd, 43 miles from Craven Arms, the line climbs at 1 in 80 to Sugar Loaf Summit, some 820 feet above sea level. At the summit is a small station, originally provided for workers and their families, at which trains stop nowadays by request. Southwards, 4 miles lie between the summit and Cynghordy station, from which northbound trains start at 1 in 60 and ease slightly to 1 in 70 as they near the summit, passing through Sugar Loaf Tunnel, 1,001 yards in length. On 30 October 1961 a pair of ex-LMS '8F' 2-8-0s approach the entrance to the tunnel with a northbound freight. *B. J. Ashworth*

Heading south down the bank from Sugar Loaf Tunnel on 20 May 1964 is Standard Class '5' 4-6-0 No 73097 with the 7.50am Craven Arms to Swansea (Victoria) train.

Today's scene, taken at roughly the same location on 6 June 1993, shows ex-LMS 'Black Five' 4-6-0 No 44769 and Standard Class 4 tank No 80079 climbing up to the summit with a Carmarthen to Shrewsbury special. Both scenes show the beauty of the area and how, over the years, the afforestation has spread. *Hugh Ballantyne/RS*

The line crosses Cynghordy viaduct (283 yards long) and enters Cynghordy station, where this view, looking south towards Llandovery, was taken on 9 April 1972. The station used to boast a passing loop, but this was taken out in the 1960s.

This was the scene at Cynghordy station on 26 April 1998, showing the newly installed platform shelter and station nameboard. *J. A. Sommerfield/RS*

Five miles south of Cynghordy the line reaches Llandovery, 60 miles from Craven Arms. It has now left the mountainous region behind and is running through gentle farmland, following the valley of the Rivers Bran and Towy. In this splendid photograph of Llandovery station, looking north about 1900, we see probably all the railway staff and, for good measure, the local police sergeant. Behind the photographer were the goods sidings and a cattle dock, which have now all gone, although some of the goods offices still remain.

On the evening of 2 May 1998 single unit No 153372 enters Llandovery with the 1733 Shrewsbury-Swansea service. The northbound platform buildings have been replaced and the footbridge has now gone, but the main station building is still intact, although now out of use. A modern crossing with lights now guards the A40 trunk road from Brecon to Carmarthen. *Lens of Sutton/RS*

After passing through Llanwrda station, which originally had staggered platforms and now has only a single platform, the line reaches Llangadog station (originally spelt Llangadock). A comparison of the 'past' picture (looking north around 1900) and the 'present' view (dated 26 April 1998) shows only the house on the left-hand side as a point of reference between them. *Lens of Sutton/RS*

The line now passes through two small stations, Glanrhyd Halt and Talley Road (both of which were closed to passenger traffic in the 1950s) before reaching the major town of Llandilo, some 71 miles from Craven Arms and once the junction for the LNWR branch to Carmarthen, which closed in 1963. From here to Pontardulais (the junction for Llanelly) the line was Great Western Railway and was used by both LNWR and GWR trains, as witnessed by this picture of ex-GWR 0-6-0 pannier tank No 7402 waiting to leave Llandilo with a Llanelly train in the late 1950s. Notice the advert for Virol, a common sight at stations in the early post-war years. On the extreme right can be seen the edge of the bay platform used by Carmarthen trains. Apart from the platforms, very little of the 'past' scene remains on 26 April 1998. *Lens of Sutton/RS*

Great Western to Pontardulais

Just under a mile from Llandilo is Ffairfach where, on the evening of 19 May 1964, ex-GWR 0-6-0PT No 8474 is seen entering the station with the 6.55pm train from Llandovery to Llanelly.

Today's view shows the rear of single unit No 153373 as it leaves Ffairfach with the 1742 Swansea to Shrewsbury service on 2 May 1998. *Hugh Ballantyne/RS*

After passing through the site of Derwydd Road station, which closed to passenger traffic in 1954, the line reaches Llandebie station. This view, taken in pre-Grouping days, shows an unidentified LNWR tank locomotive on a southbound local train.

The 'present' view, taken from the same vantage point on 2 May 1998, shows the crossing and the edge of the station. The signal box lasted until 1985, but the passing loop, etc, went in the 1960s. *Lens of Sutton/RS*

Some 2 miles from Llandebie and 77½ miles from Craven Arms is Ammanford station, which from 1960 to 1973 was known as Ammanford & Tirydail; as can be seen in this picture, taken on 9 April 1972, the signal box that controlled the crossing at the northern end of the small station was known as Tirydail Station.

On 2 May 1998, at the same crossing, the box has gone and traffic signals now control the crossing. Just north of the station was the junction for the line than ran west to Tumble.

From now onwards the character of the line changes, and instead of farmland it runs through many mining areas, although today most of the South Wales mines have been closed. *J. A. Sommerfield/RS*

Pantyffynnon was the junction for the line running north-eastwards to Brynamman. This view of the junction station, looking north, was taken in the 1950s, with the Brynamman line curving away to the right.

The line to Brynamman closed to passengers many years ago, but the 2 May 1998 view clearly shows the line, which was still in industrial use (to Abernant) until a few years ago. The only platform now remaining is the southbound one, which looks very similar to the 'past' view, complete with semaphore signals. The signal box controlling this once-busy junction is still in use, and is situated south of the station on the eastern side of the line. *Lens of Sutton/RS*

Into Swansea

Nowadays, Central Wales Line trains to Swansea run via Llanelly (where a reversal is necessary) then via the Paddington main line, but for the purpose of this book we take the original route to Swansea, which left the Llanelly line at Pontardulais and ran south-eastwards via the Gower Peninsula to the original terminus of the line at Swansea (Victoria). This scene at Pontardulais Junction, taken in the 1950s, shows ex-LMS Fowler 2-6-4T No 42385 entering the station with an evening train for Swansea.

All that remains today at Pontardulais (83½ miles from Craven Arms) is a single platform. On 2 May 1998 unit No 153303 is seen arriving at that platform with the 1311 from Shrewsbury to Llanelly and Swansea. The photograph was taken from the trackbed of the old Swansea line. *Lens of Sutton/RS*

Leaving the joint station at Pontardulais, the line to Swansea was once again LNWR and also double track. This view of the remains of Gorseinon station, looking north towards Pontardulais, was taken on 9 April 1972, eight years after the closure of this section of the line in 1964.

Today, in the same view taken on 2 May 1998, nothing at all remains to remind us that there was once a railway in this area. *J. A. Sommerfield/RS*

Some 5 miles south of Pontardulais and 88½ miles from Craven Arms was Gowerton LNWR station, situated adjacent to and to the south of Gowerton GWR station (on the Paddington-Swansea-Carmarthen route). In 1950 the former LNWR station became Gowerton South, and the ex-GWR one became Gowerton North. Gowerton was also the junction for the branch to Llanmorlais, and this picture, taken in LNWR days, shows the branch curving away westwards to the left, and the Central Wales Line on the right to Pontardulais and the north. Note the wooden station buildings and the LNWR lower-quadrant signals.

On 2 May 1998 all that remains of Gowerton station is the trackbed, which now forms a pleasant walkway. *Lens of Sutton/RS*

After passing through Dunvant station, where there were sidings and a spur to serve the local collieries, etc, the line entered the attractive station of Killay, just under 5 miles from the terminus at Swansea. This view, looking westwards, dates from LNWR days.

In this picture, taken on 2 May 1998, the station house can be glimpsed on the left; it is now a public house. The trackbed is also still visible. *J. A. Peden collection/RS*

The line next descended to Mumbles Road station, then headed eastwards along the Gower coast to Swansea, where it also parallelled the famous Swansea & Mumbles electric tramway. This view of Mumbles Road station, looking north-westwards, was, like the Killay picture, taken in pre-Grouping days.

Only the hillside in today's view, taken on 2 May 1998, and perhaps part of the trackbed – now a cycle track – allow any comparison with the LNWR-era view. To the left of the picture, out of sight, is the preserved electric powerhouse of the Mumbles tramway. *Lens of Sutton/RS*

After Mumbles Road, we reach the penultimate station on the line – Swansea Bay, 94¾ miles from Craven Arms and a mile from Swansea (Victoria). On 19 May 1964 (a few weeks before the closure of this section of the line to passenger traffic in June of that year) ex-GWR 0-6-0PT No 3671 leaves Swansea Bay station with the 4.15pm local train from Swansea (Victoria) to Pontardulais. Note the sand on this westbound platform, the line now running right by the sea.

Today's picture, taken on 2 May 1998, shows that the trackbed is now a cycle track. The footbridge to the beach on the right-hand side can also be seen in the 'past' picture, just beyond the station footbridge. This footbridge also crosses over the Mumbles road and the electric tramway, which was situated between the road and the railway line. Almost opposite the station site is the Swansea cricket and rugby football ground where, in 1968, the legendary Gary Sobers (playing for Nottinghamshire) hit Glamorgan bowler Malcolm Nash for six sixes in one six-ball over. *Hugh Ballantyne/RS*

Just before arriving at Swansea (Victoria) the line passed by Paxton Street shed (south of the line) where this view of ex-LMS 'Jinty' 0-6-0 tank No 47478 was taken on 14 July 1957. On the left is an ex-LMS 2-6-4 tank and just behind the 'Jinty' is Standard Class '4' 4-6-0 No 75022. Paxton Street was the Central Wales Line's biggest shed, its allocation being up to 50 locomotives in its heyday.

On 2 May 1998 the shed site plays host to the recently built County Hall. On the right, through the arch under the building, can be seen the embankment that carried the line. *Industrial Railway Society, Brian Webb collection/RS*

Journey's end is the terminus of the line at Swansea (Victoria), which was originally owned by the Llanelly Railway until taken over by the LNWR in 1873, still in an unfinished state, and finally completed in 1882, some 11 years after the start of the building in 1871. On 10 June 1960 ex-LMS 'Black Five' 4-6-0 No 45283 is ready to depart with the 10.25am to Shrewsbury. On the right, ex-GWR 0-6-0PT No 4650 shunts in the sidings. Above the pannier tank can be seen the GWR line connecting the South Dock with the North Dock and other GWR lines. There was also a connection from Victoria station via the right-hand sidings to the GWR and Swansea Harbour Trust lines. Note the large goods shed on the left.

The line from Pontardulais to Swansea (Victoria) closed to passenger traffic on 13 June 1964, but the goods yard remained in use until October 1965, access being via the high-level GWR line from Swansea (High Street). In the 'present' view, taken on 2 May 1998, only the background hills and the tower on the left-hand skyline identify this as the same location as the 'past' picture. A car park and leisure centre (beyond which is the Dylan Thomas Theatre) occupy the bulk of the station site. Central Wales trains now terminate at the former GWR Swansea (High Street) station, approaching via Llanelly and the Paddington main line. *Hugh Ballantyne/RS*

Before we leave Swansea and the Central Wales Line, it is appropriate to include this 10 June 1960 photograph of Swansea & Mumbles tram No 2 having its upper deck dismantled at York Street bridge (to the east of Victoria station) prior to being transported to Leeds for preservation.

This is the site of York Road bridge on 2 May 1998 (in the foreground is Victoria Road) with, obligingly, a passing horse and carriage! *Hugh Ballantyne/RS*

INDEX OF LOCATIONS